From **One Heart**
To **Another**

Poetry by a Grieving Mother
LYNN VINCENT

Copyright ©2025 by Lynn Vincent
First Edition: December 2025
www.lynnvincent.com.au
Lilly Pilly *Grace* Publishing

All rights reserved.

No portion of this book may be reproduced, distributed, or transmitted in any form or by any means, including but not limited to, photocopying, recording, for any artificial intelligence (AI) use or purposes or training, or other electronic or mechanical methods, without the prior written permission of the author, except as permitted by U.S. and Australian copyright law. For permission requests, please contact Lynn Vincent at hello@lynnvincent.com.au

This book is not intended as a substitute for the medical recommendations of physicians, mental health professionals, or any other health care providers. It is sold with the understanding that neither the author nor the publisher is engaged in rendering any medical or professional services. Any advice and strategies contained herein may not be suitable for your situation. You should consult with a professional when appropriate. Neither the publisher nor the author shall be liable for any loss or damages, including but not limited to financial, special, incidental, consequential, personal, or other damages.

ISBN: 978-1-7642496-0-7 (print book)
Book Cover Art & Illustrations by Lisa-Marie Vecchio (Lisa Dot Design)

NATIONAL
LIBRARY
OF AUSTRALIA

In Memoriam

Dorian Vincent

11.12.23 – 16.07.24

Our precious boy. Our gift from God.

Contents

Introduction	i
PART 1 – Stages of Grief	1
Denial:	5
You Should Still Be Here	8
Waiting On A Miracle	9
Anger:	11
I'm Angry	14
Irrationally So	15
Bargaining:	17
Never Enough	20
What If	21
Depression:	23
No More Joy	27
Without You	28
Acceptance:	31
Accepted	33
Wait For Me	34

PART 2 – **From One Heart To Another**	37

DORIAN	39
Precious Boy	40
From One Heart To Another	42
Your Sibling, I Will Always Be	43

PART 3 – **Dear Everyone Else**	45

How I Feel	50
How Dare You	52
Not The Same	54
You Don't Know	55
Say Their Name	56
To My Friends Who Remain	57

PART 4 – **Loss Before, or At Birth**	59

Poppy	62
Stolen	63
After	64
Rainbow	65

PART 5 – **Milestones**	67

You Should've Been One Today	70
Two Precious For This Earth	72
Mother's Day	73
Christmas	74
One Year Without You	75
Milestones We Never Asked For	76

PART 6 – **Faith Musings** 79

Beauty From Ashes 83
You Said 84
Restoration – Your Way 86
Yours, Not Mine 88
My Reason 89

PART 7 – **Moving On (But Never Gone)** 91

Holding On 93
Moving On 94
Never Gone 96
One Day 97
My Hopes For You 98

Afterword 100
Acknowledgements 102
About the Author 104

Introduction

I'd always wanted to be a mother, but my motherhood journey has never gone as expected or hoped. I miscarried my first; had a beautiful neurodivergent boy who challenges everything I thought I knew about motherhood; had another suspected miscarriage; had my second little boy who decided to challenge me in completely different ways to his brother; then found out less than a year later that I had miraculously fallen pregnant again with another boy.

This pregnancy wasn't planned. I say it was miraculous because I've never been able to conceive and carry a pregnancy to term without being on medication. Yet there we were almost eight weeks in. To say we were shocked was an understatement. It was definitely a stressful discovery just trying to work out the logistics of how this was going to affect our lives. However, being a miraculous pregnancy, I decided to put my trust in God that He would take care of everything.

But just as we had processed the news and were starting to get excited about this final piece to our family puzzle, we found out that our little boy's heart hadn't formed properly. He was diagnosed with multiple rare cardiac complications, and a few people even advised me to terminate the pregnancy. But in faith, I refused. This began an even more stressful and frightening time, as we tried to get through the pregnancy without knowing what might happen – that's if we even made it to the birth.

It was an incredible test of faith, but our little boy, Dorian, defied all odds and medical expectations. He was born happy, healthy, and without requiring any surgical interventions or life supports. In fact, he was discharged from NICU within a week, and continued to defy the odds, growing into a beautiful and peaceful soul – the very essence of joy – despite a life filled with constant hospital appointments, medical reviews, and numerous health precautions.

Dorian remained healthy and strong, thriving on his own without interventions, until one day in July 2024. He passed away suddenly and unexpectedly at just seven months old, following a trip to ED because of reasons that we may never fully know on this earth. Between that and my history of depression, anxiety, and mental health illness, I really should not be standing here today, let alone functioning. But by God's grace, I am.

Losing your child is every parent's worst fear – you can't possibly imagine it, and you don't even want to try! This fear was now my reality. What made it even harder was discovering that grief, and especially grief over a child lost, is an incredibly lonely journey. Unless they've been through it before, other people will never understand what you're going through, no matter how much they try. It's not the same as losing a parent or a partner, although there will be people who think it is.

Now, writing has always been a creative outlet and mental health therapy for me, even as a child. As a teen, I'd channel my "depression" into writing poetry – little did I know then what true depression would be like! It was my dream to write and publish a book one day, but that dream went from "by the time I'm 16" to "18" to "21" to "one day". After I graduated university, working life became so busy that I stopped writing, until I had to figure out what to say at Dorian's memorial.

In one day, I poured my heart out into three different poems. This not only reignited my passion for writing and my dream to write a book – it also led me to this one: a collection of poems written in my grief, to help me process and navigate the journey. A space to release emotions that sometimes felt too big or too difficult for me to voice out loud. A space that might dare me to dream once again, and to hope that one day, I might find healing for my heart.

From One Heart To Another is truly a heart-project – it holds so much love and meaning within. Even the title alone carries deep significance. It represents Dorian's heart: once malformed and defective here on earth, now made whole in heaven. It represents my mum-heart: once full of hope, now heartbroken – yet despite that, still waiting for God to take the pieces and restore them. And it also represents the poetry itself: flowing from my heart and reaching out to yours – to the hearts of other mums, parents, grandparents, and others who have known the pain of losing a child, or even just the sorrow of losing a loved one.

Being a poetry book, I'm aware that it may be unlikely that anyone will sit down and read it all in one go. Therefore, I've decided to lay out my poems in sections. Each section will take you on its own journey, but all together and read in order, I hope this book in its entirety may also take you on another journey - one which reflects how grief isn't linear. That said, you certainly don't have to read it in the order I've set out.

The sections will hopefully make it easier for you to find something that suits your mood and needs each time you pick up this book. Some sections may not feel relevant to you right now, so feel free to skip them for the moment. However, I hope you will eventually come back to them when you're ready and give them a chance. While they may not resonate personally, I like to think they might help us become more aware of someone else's situation and experience. Then through that awareness, maybe we can support them just a little better.

However you decide to read this book, it is my hope that this collection of poems helps you to feel seen - a little more understood, a little less crazy, and most importantly, a little less alone. I hope these poems resonate with you. That they help you navigate your grief journey by giving a voice to your pain, the courage to face other people (and permission to place boundaries to protect yourself if you need to), and the encouragement to hope again.

Most of all, I hope this book inspires you to find purpose in your pain - so you can keep going, and live a full, meaningful life despite your grief.

Stages of Grief

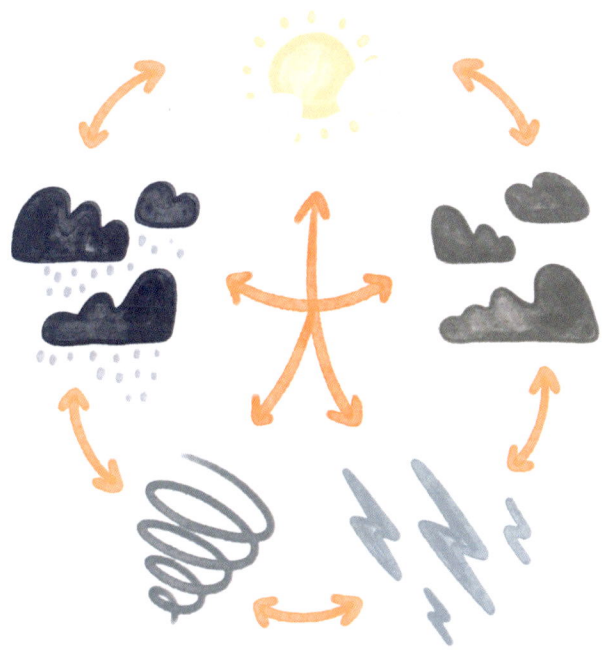

Stages of Grief

I believe everyone has heard of the five stages of grief: *denial, anger, bargaining, depression,* and *acceptance*. But what most people might not realise is that these stages aren't linear.

I've found that grief is like a cycle; endless. Each stage is connected to all the other stages, and there's no pattern – no rhyme or reason. Sometimes, I'm stuck in one stage for several days. Sometimes, I go through all five stages in no set order…all in the same hour!

Grief is the rollercoaster you never wanted to be on. You're dragged in, strapped down, and taken along for the ride, with absolutely no control over anything, including when you get off. There is no set timeline or timeframe for your grief journey, and it will look very different from mine or anyone else's. Grief is *not* "one size fits all".

Even though I've set out this section of poems in what might seem like a linear order based on the five stages of grief, I want you to know that reality rarely follows that path. Whatever you are feeling – it's okay. You're not crazy. You're human.

This is your grief journey. Don't let anyone plan the

itinerary for you. Your way, your time. That said, I do want to note that I believe there is a difference between living your grief journey on your own terms, and allowing yourself to stay stuck in the downward spiral forever.

I know there will be times when you don't feel like interacting with anyone, but I wouldn't recommend doing your entire grief journey alone. Even if you feel like nobody around you understands, I really want to encourage you to find at least one person to talk to - whether it's a counsellor, a therapist, or even calling one of those free hotlines.

This is your grief journey, but you don't have to walk it alone. You are not alone – let others walk beside you.

Denial

- A mind fog – like you're in a dream or removed from the situation
- Numbness
- Panic attacks: tingling, tremors, dizziness, heart pounding, nausea
- Hope
- Mental blackouts and poor recall memory
- Masking of emotions and how you're faring
- Disbelief about what has happened

Denial

In the early days and weeks of grief, denial for me was mostly a mind fog. I was functioning on autopilot, and only because I had two other boys to look after – otherwise, I would have probably stayed in bed all day. I didn't want to think, because thinking just meant more pain. But even while trying to shut my mind, the pain was still there.

I remember feeling numb and cold – so very cold. And I would have panic attacks. My body and mind had gone through the worst trauma it had ever experienced, and now any additional perceived threat (whether it was real or not) would send my body into shut-down mode. My panic attacks would begin with a sharp, tingling numbness, which would lead to shakes and tremors. I'd start to feel dizzy – I've never fainted before, but I imagine this is what it would feel like right before you pass out. My heart would be racing and pounding. Sometimes, I felt like I wanted to vomit.

The underlying root of my denial came from my faith. I had a God who could perform miracles, who *had* performed miracles. A God who had healed and raised many from the dead. This was not how our story was supposed to go. Surely God didn't give me a miraculous conception, followed by a miraculous birth and a miraculous life for Dorian, only for our story to end this way. Dorian's heart was supposed to be miraculously healed, and he was supposed to live a long, miraculous, and blessed life – a testimony of God's power.

My state of denial clung to this hope that it was not truly the end. That this was just a test of my faith. That God would bring Dorian back to me, and *that* would be the ultimate miracle and testimony. In fact, I stayed in denial right until the cremation, but that's a story for another time.

Now, my denial presents in slightly different ways. Some days, it's like I'm in a dream, or rather, a nightmare – it can feel like I've been removed from the situation, and I'm just watching it play out. My mind still gets foggy at times. It doesn't work like it used to, and sometimes, I experience mental blackouts and have trouble recalling simple things.

Most of the denial presents as masking of how I actually feel and how I'm really faring. I find myself doing this around most people to avoid awkwardness and unexpected triggers. I try to keep busy and distract myself so I can push my feelings to the back of my mind but this usually ends in a mental breakdown so I wouldn't recommend it.

However, the most painful presentation of my denial is a disbelief that this really happened. That I *actually* lost my son. And with it, there's always shock at how much and how quickly time has flown. That we've now been without Dorian for longer than we got to keep him.

You Should Still Be Here

This does not seem real,
You should still be here.
How could this have happened?
A parent's biggest fear.

The world couldn't be this cruel,
To take this child of mine.
Surely, I must be dreaming.
How can life be so unkind?

Wake me from this nightmare,
And let me find you near.
Surely this cannot be real,
You should still be here.

This cannot be real; tell me,
This is just not real.
You should still be here, my precious.
This should not be real.

Waiting On A Miracle

I'm still waiting on a miracle,
I'm still hoping we've been misled.
A part of me still believes,
God will raise you from the dead.

Jesus brought back the widow's son,
A leader's daughter, and Lazarus of Bethany.
I'm still waiting on a miracle,
That He'll bring you back to me.

This wasn't supposed to be your story,
Things weren't meant to end this way.
I'm still waiting on a miracle,
Death should not have the final say.

I'm still waiting on a miracle,
Surely this future isn't set.
I'm still waiting for my miracle,
This can't be over yet.

Anger

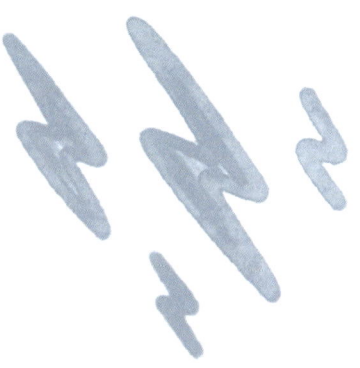

- Angry, furious, mad – like a volcano about to explode
- Wanting to scream and shout, to stomp, hit, or punch something
- Wanting to pass some of your pain on to something or someone else
- Bitterness, resentment, and blame
- Feeling like a failure
- Hurt and betrayal

Anger

Red, hot, furious, mad. Those are the words most of us would think of when asked to describe anger. My oldest son's favourite way of describing it is like a volcano about to explode – and it's so accurate! The anger builds up inside you, and when it gets too much, you need to let it out, so you explode. That comes out as shouting, stomping, hitting, or punching something – you're essentially trying to pass some of your pain on to something or someone else.

Yes, I felt all those things. At everything, and everyone. My anger was bitter and resentful – it looked for people to blame: the ED team, the head paediatrician that evening, the cardiac team. But most of all, I blamed myself because I felt like I'd failed. I should have done more. I should have followed my gut. I let my child down.

After what I shared about my denial stage, most people would think that I'd also be angry at God. But I remember telling some people in the week of Dorian's passing that I wasn't. That I *couldn't* be angry at God, because how could I question His will when I know that He is good?

Looking back now, I believe I was thinking of anger in the usual ways that I've just talked about. But one thing

I've realised is that anger doesn't always look red-hot. Sometimes, anger can come in the form of hurt and betrayal. I discovered this when I dug deeper into the blame and resentment I had for those people mentioned above. I realised the underlying cause of those feelings was that I felt betrayed by them. Because they should have done things differently. Because they should have known better.

And that's when I realised: maybe, I was angry at God too. Not in the red-hot way, but in the hurt and betrayed way. Because I'd expected God to heal, to fix, to bring Dorian back – but He didn't. Because I'd trusted God, but He still allowed this horrible thing to happen to me.

Despite my anger, I haven't let it affect my faith – I'm lucky that I have a God who understands grief and allows me my moments of anger. And yes, I still have moments of anger, blame, resentment, and hurt towards everyone, including myself.

However, I choose to work on forgiveness and healing. Personally, I believe that of all the five stages, anger is the most detrimental – not just for my own wellbeing, but also the people around me whom I love. Therefore, while I believe it's okay to have moments of anger, I work hard not to stay angry and bitter. I'm trying to let it go.

I'm Angry

I'm angry because it isn't fair.
Haven't I suffered enough?
I've been through so much already,
Why must my life be so rough?

I'm angry I can't change the past,
I'm filled with all this regret.
It would've been different if I had known,
That was all the time we'd get.

I'm angry at the Mum I was.
I failed; I let you down.
Maybe if I had trusted my gut,
You would still be around.

I'm angry because this isn't right,
But there's nothing I can do.
No parent should have to mourn their child,
I should have gone before you.

I'm angry because it hurts so much,
I'm angry because I'm sad.
I'm angry because I'm powerless,
I'm angry, furious, mad.

Irrationally So

I am just so angry –
Irrationally so.
Angry just at everything,
And everyone I know.

And even as I lash out,
I know that I should stop.
But the anger just keeps building –
It grows until I pop.

I'm angry and I'm furious,
And I don't know the reason why,
Or who or what I'm angry at –
I just want to scream and cry.

I don't understand this anger,
That my grief seems to have woken.
Or maybe I'm just angry at myself –
I'm angry because I feel broken.

I am just so angry –
Irrationally so.
But I don't want this anger,
I want to let it go.

Bargaining

- A mental spiral
- A whirlwind of thoughts: "what if"; "maybe"; "should've/could've/would've"
- Wondering why
- Wondering what you did wrong or if you're being "punished"

Bargaining

I found this stage of grief to be quite dangerous in the sense that if I wasn't careful, I'd wind up stuck in an endless spiral of thoughts.

"What if…"
"Maybe…"
"I should/could/would have…"
"Why did/didn't I…"

That's the whirlwind of thoughts that come with the bargaining stage of grief. And overlying these questions is the ultimate question: *WHY?*

I remember thinking that it must have been something I did wrong. That maybe I was being punished. That I must be a horrible person to have such a horrible thing happen to me. It didn't help that I felt some people were insinuating this as well.

Truthfully, there are some days when I still worry and wonder about this. There are also many days when I still go through the mental spiral and whirlwind of questions. And I don't believe I will ever stop asking *why*.

However, I am lucky that I have my faith to fall back on.

Because my God is the reason that my spirals always come to an end. And at that end, I find a simple truth that I keep reminding myself: God is good, and He works all things for good.

At the end of the day, my faith reminds me that those questions above would all have led to the same answer: that nothing would have made a difference. Because if God wanted to save my son, He would have. But He didn't.

I don't understand why, and I may never get an answer while I'm on earth. But even though I still have mental spirals, even though I will always wonder why, I choose instead to focus on "what now". This was something I first heard back in 2022 from Karolina Gunsser (now Grant), and it has stuck with me ever since. Because you may never get an answer to "why", but you can always find an answer to "what now".

Never Enough

I wish we could've had just one more night.
I would've stayed up all night and held you tight,
But it still wouldn't have been enough.

If only we could've had just one more day.
I'd forget about chores and work, and we'd just play,
But it still wouldn't have been enough.

Forget one more week, a month, or a year,
I'd take even another minute with you, my dear,
But it still wouldn't have been enough.

I've never wished for anything so badly before,
But even if I'd gotten all that time and more,
It still wouldn't have been enough.

No, it would always be never enough.

What If

There are so many 'what ifs',
They constantly churn inside my mind.
I imagine each possibility, I play out each scenario,
Looking for answers I'll never find.

It's hard not to blame myself,
Or think that it was something I did wrong.
What if I'd done this, or if I hadn't done that,
Would you still be here growing strong?

Memories of that day plague my mind,
And fill me with anger, guilt, and regret.
What if I'd done things differently?
Could I have avoided this trauma and threat?

Not a day goes by where I don't cry,
Where I'm not filled with 'what ifs' and 'whys',
Wondering why we had to say goodbye,
Wishing I could look into your eyes.

Of all the paths my life could have gone,
I never thought it would take this track.
Now I'm just left with the 'what ifs',
But 'what ifs' can't bring you back.

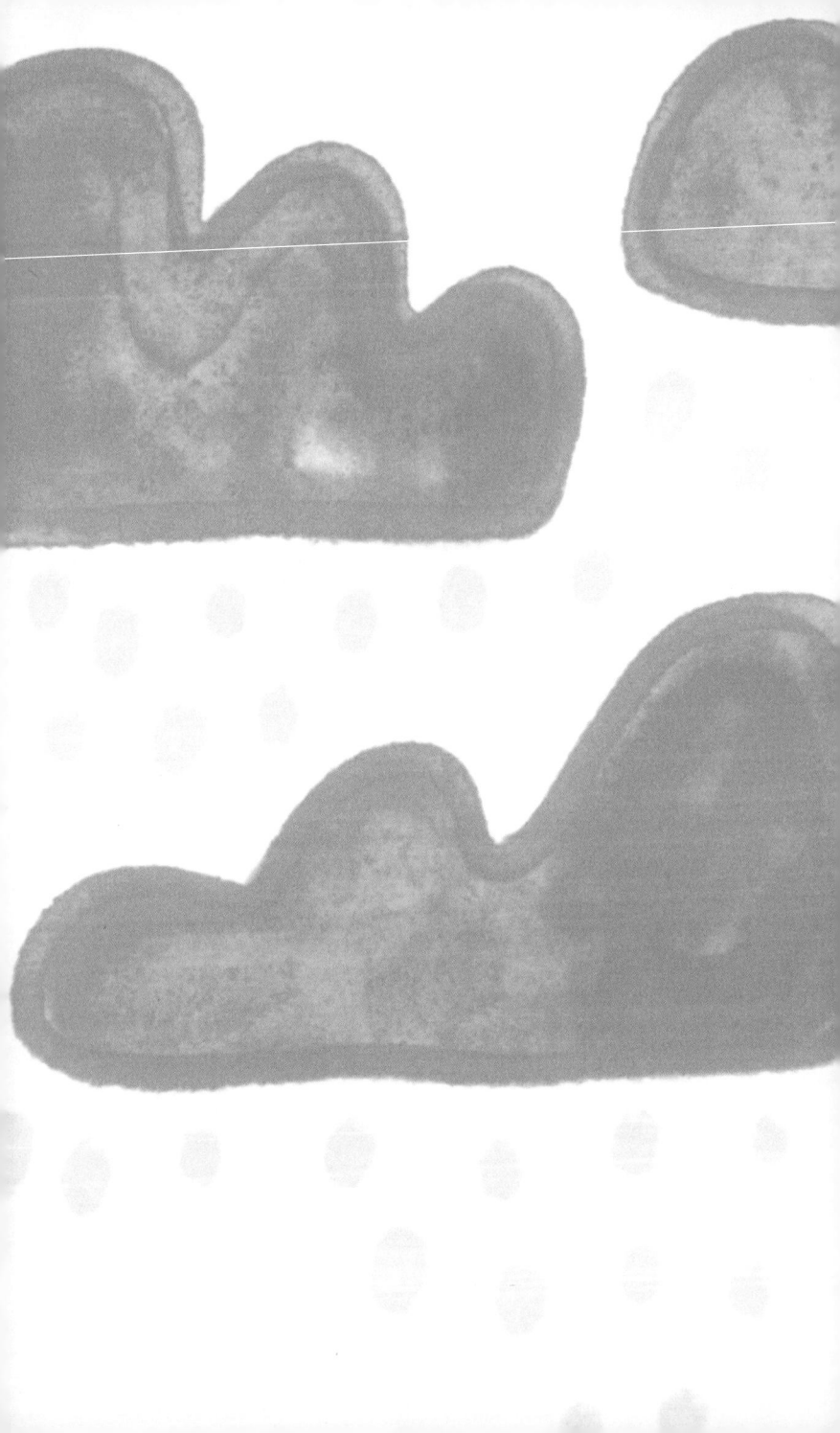

Depression

- Not the same person you were before
- Things you loved no longer bring you joy
- Loss of appetite – food might taste different
- Not wanting to leave bed, couch, or house
- Not wanting to do anything
- Loss of will and motivation – just existing
- Sorrow, tears, and breakdowns
- Chilling numbness, pain, and hurt
- Physical signs and symptoms: weight loss/gain, hair loss, insomnia, health issues
- Comes and goes in waves – rarely with a warning
- Suicidal thoughts and inclinations*

Depression

Depression and I go way back. In hindsight, I've probably had several episodes of depression since my teenage years, including my first encounter with grief when the only grandfather I'd ever known passed away.

However, the most notable episode (prior to Dorian's passing) was in 2017, when I spent most of the year battling depression, anxiety, and mental health illness. Although I never figured out what triggered it, and although whatever the trigger was could never compare to that of losing my son, the signs and the symptoms of depression were the same. Grief only amplified them.

Depression and grief change you. You're not the person you were before. I found that many things I loved no longer brought me joy. Even food no longer tasted the same – not that I had much of an appetite anyway! It was hard for me to leave the bed or couch, let alone the house! I didn't really want to do anything – except maybe binge-watch movies or TV shows because they served as a mind-numbing distraction, and the noise helped me feel less alone.

I lost the will and motivation for most things – I was basically just existing. However, I have to say that this was the one symptom of depression that wasn't necessarily amplified for me in grief. However, I believe this was only because I still had two young children who needed me, compared to 2017, which was pre-children.

Depression isn't just sorrow, tears, and breakdowns. There's also a chilling numbness to it – except with grief, that numbness still isn't enough to block out the pain and hurt. There are also the physical signs and symptoms of depression: weight loss/gain, hair loss, insomnia, just to name a few. These are usually associated to the stress your body is under, and as we all know, stress can also lead to a myriad of problems and health issues.

Something I realised about depression is that it can come and go in waves. Some days, you're wading in the shallows – you feel okay, you're able to keep your head up, and maybe even function normally. Other days, the wave crashes down right on top of you and you're struggling to figure out which way is up. Unfortunately, you rarely get a warning before this happens. I've found that unexpected triggers are the worst, and often take me longer to recover from.

*Finally, I feel it would be remiss of me not to mention suicidal thoughts and inclinations, despite never having experienced these myself. All I can say is, please, please, *please* talk to someone, preferably a trained professional, if you're feeling this way. In fact, I would strongly encourage seeing a qualified counsellor, psychologist, or psychiatrist for your grief, regardless! I can't express how much this has helped me – having a safe, no-judgement space to voice my thoughts and feelings.

Remember, you are not alone, no matter how loudly your mind tries to scream this at you. There is always light in the darkness – sometimes it just takes someone else to find the match and light it.

No More Joy

I'm not the person I once was,
There's no joy left anymore.
Sure, I might smile and laugh,
But it's not like it was before.

All the things I used to love,
No longer bring me joy.
The world is now a different place,
Without my precious boy.

Even foods I used to eat,
No longer taste the same.
Nothing seems to bring me joy,
There's only grief to blame.

I'm not the person I used to be,
After everything I've been through.
The world's a greyer, dimmer place,
There's no more joy without you.

Without You

It just doesn't feel right without you –
It's too quiet and yet too loud.
It's like the world I live in now,
Has been covered by a shroud.

Without you, there's no warmth anymore,
I just constantly feel numb and cold.
It's strange without you in my arms,
To kiss, to cuddle, to hold.

You should be snuggled against me,
As you go down for your nap.
You should be cooing and babbling,
As you bounce up and down on my lap.

You should be glued to my side,
Attached as I go about my day,
Always demanding attention,
Wanting to feed and to play.

But now my days feel so empty,
And I've got all this time just for me –
Something I longed for, but not anymore,
I'd rather have you than be free.

Without you, there's a hole inside me,
A pain that's so raw and unreal.
And no matter just how much time passes,
These wounds can and will never heal.

It just doesn't feel right without you –
There's too much sorrow and pain.
No, it'll never feel right without you.
No, it'll never be right again.

Acceptance

- Accepting reality - that your loved one is gone, and nothing can ever change that
- Accepting that grief will always be part of your life
- Can coexist with the other stages of grief
- First step towards healing
- Choosing to keep going despite everything

Acceptance

People often think that acceptance is the final stage of grief. That acceptance means you're healed. But I don't believe that to be true. For me, this stage of grief is about accepting reality. That my precious boy is gone, and nothing can ever change that. It's about accepting that grief is part of my life now. That I will carry grief with me till the day I die.

I've found that you can accept these things, but that doesn't mean you're healed or that you will no longer experience the other stages of grief. In fact, I believe that acceptance is only the first step towards healing. Unfortunately, healing is a journey with an immeasurable number of steps in a maze with no map to guide you. But that's okay – I can accept that healing will take time, and that I may never be whole again.

Mostly, acceptance to me is choosing to keep going despite all that has happened. I choose to keep running the race set before me. I choose to find purpose in my pain. I choose to be a light in the darkness.

Above all, I choose to live a life that Dorian would be proud of, and to ensure his legacy carries on. Dorian touched the hearts of so many people in his short time on earth – I will ensure our story keeps touching lives long after we're both gone.

Accepted

I've accepted my little one is gone,
There is no coming back.
I'll have to live forevermore,
Knowing there's a child I lack.

I've accepted life will always be,
A little emptier and less fulfilled.
I'm trying to put myself back together,
But there are parts I can never rebuild.

I've accepted I will always be,
A little bit broken; never whole again.
There's a piece of my heart missing,
A broken link in my family chain.

I've accepted healing will take time,
It's a journey I may never complete.
But if I can keep standing and living life,
At least I can be proud of that feat.

Wait for Me

Wait for me, my little one,
I'll see you once again.
When next we meet, there'll just be peace,
And tears of joy, not pain.

I'm not quite sure how long I'll take,
But I'm coming, have no fear.
If I could, I'd come right now,
But I'm still needed here.

That doesn't mean I won't think of you,
Every hour of every day.
I'll miss and love you forevermore,
So much more than words can say.

I'm not sure if I will ever stop,
Wondering or asking why –
Why you had to leave so soon,
Why it had to be goodbye.

But although we're not together now,
We'll never be truly apart.
Your name and memory will never fade,
You'll always be in my heart.

And I'll be sure to tell your story,
With every chance I get.
I'll ensure your legacy carries on,
I'll let no one forget.

And when my time on earth is finally up,
I know I won't complain,
Because I'll get to be with you,
And hold you once again.

So just wait, my little one,
For when my race here is run.
Wait for me, my little one,
Our story's not yet done.

From One Heart to Another

From One Heart To Another

As I wrote in the introduction, this book, *From One Heart To Another,* is very much a heart-project and holds so much love and meaning within it. Right at the heart of this book is the love I have for my precious son, Dorian, who was taken from this earth far too soon. And yet, this book will never be enough to demonstrate the depth of my feelings: my love for him and the grief from losing him.

This titular section contains my Dorian-centred pieces - the things I wish I could say to him, the things I hope he knew, and a very special poem at the end: what I imagine he'd tell his brothers if he could. Of all the sections in this book, I feel this one comes closest to depicting the full extent of my love and my pain. It is my feelings laid bare, my love on display, my mind wrestling with itself, and some of my trauma unpacked.

This section is my heart – raw, open, and served unfiltered on a platter.

DORIAN

Dorian, my precious boy, I miss you every day.
One question I'll never stop asking is why you couldn't stay.
Racking my brain, wondering why it had to be this way.
If I could get you back, is there a price I wouldn't pay?
At the end of the day, all I can do is accept our fate and pray.
Next time we meet, we'll have forever, and all will be okay.

Despite how much time has passed, I will never forget you.
Often, I think of everything we've been through.
Recalling your cuddles, your laughs, everything you'd do.
I wish I could've seen the man you'd have grown into.
All my life now I'll wait to be reunited with you.
Next time we meet, we'll get that happy ending we were due.

Precious Boy

Your oldest brother was darling,
Your second brother was sweet,
But you, my beautiful boy, were precious –
The most precious boy I ever did meet.

It's not that you were better,
Or that I loved you more,
But you passed when you were just a babe,
Still so innocent, still pure.

We went through so much together,
Since I realised you were in my belly.
I never stopped believing in you,
And you never ceased to amaze me.

I hope you had a happy life with us –
I worry I let you down.
I wish I had done more with you,
And made the most of the time you were around.

Even if I couldn't have made a difference,
Even if God's will would have always prevailed,
I should have fought for you harder.
I should have put you first; I failed.

I hope you knew that we were there.
I hope you weren't scared or in pain.
I hope you know that we'll always love you.
I hope one day we'll all be together again.

Until then, you will always be remembered:
Our precious Dorian, the essence of joy,
Our miracle, our little lion, our fighter,
Our gift from God, our precious boy.

From One Heart To Another

The only thing harder than having you go,
Is not having an answer for why it had to be so.

The world has tried to find the reason why,
But the answers they give just don't satisfy.

Only God knows why He had to take you back,
Before He healed your heart and gave it all it lacked.

I wish it were different but He's in control.
At least now you've got a heart that's whole.

I've also gone from one heart to another –
From a heart of hope to a heartbroken mother.

But with God's grace, not my own accord,
He'll transform my heart of grief to a heart restored.

And while I wait for that, I'll keep telling our story,
Of my journey with grief, of your life, my precious Dori.

And as I keep sharing the truths from my heart,
We might touch the hearts of others through my works of art.

Then love may flow from one heart to another,
Through the writings and poetry of a grieving mother.

Your Sibling, I Will Always Be

I'm sorry that I couldn't stay,
That I can't join in when you play,
That I can't help you look for beetles and bugs,
Or be part of our family cuddles and hugs.
I'm sorry I can't be there with you,
To cheer you up when you've got the flu,
Or to celebrate on Christmas Day,
Or sing you Happy Birthday and shout, "Hooray!"
I know you're sad because it isn't fair,
That I'm not around and can't be there.
I would've stayed with you if I could,
But sometimes things don't go as they should.
But I'm watching you from here in heaven,
I promise I won't miss out on even a second.
I'm really sorry that I couldn't stay,
But know that I'm with you every day,
In your head and in your heart,
Nobody can ever keep us apart.
Your sibling, I will always be,
We'll always, always be family.

Dear Everyone Else

Dear Everyone Else,

Grief is hard enough to process for the person going through it, let alone someone who has never experienced grief. And even if they have experienced grief, no two experiences are ever the same. Losing a child is very different from losing a parent or a spouse, and even the grief from losing one child is completely different from that of losing a different child (something I'll share a bit more about in the next section of this book 'Loss Before/ At Birth'). Even my grief is different from that of my husband's, despite it being over the same child – *our* child.

I believe this is one of the reasons why grief is so isolating – you feel like nobody can truly understand what you're going through. Another reason is that people just don't know what to say or how to act around you, especially when you're grieving over a child. I don't blame them. When someone passes from old age, it's sad but they've lived a long life, and that sort of death is "expected". When someone passes after battling sickness, it's sad but people will say that at least it's a mercy they weren't suffering anymore. But when a child passes – no matter the reason – what do you say to that?

In my experience, I found that most people ended up split into these groups:

1. People who tried to say the right thing (even if they didn't);
2. People who made it all about them;
3. People who were amazingly grief aware;
4. People who stayed quiet or disappeared.

For me, the hardest group to interact with was the first group. I knew their hearts were in the right place. I can sense the awkwardness that sometimes appears as they try to find the right words; I can feel their horror, shock, and pity engulfing me. I hold no blame or anger towards this group – after all, they're trying their best in a seemingly impossible and hopeless situation.

But it can be emotionally draining for me to keep my mask on when sometimes their words or actions feel like knives to the heart. However, in time, my skin has become thicker, I've learnt to protect my heart better, and I'm perfecting the mask I wear.

The most surprising thing about the second group was that it included some unexpected people – people who were supposed to be close to us; people who we thought would be supportive and understanding. Unfortunately, instead they made our grief about them. I won't deny that there was some anger towards this group, but I think it was born mostly out of shock and disbelief that people could be so insensitive. Again though, I've learnt to deal with this in time. My anger has mostly ebbed, and I try to look on the bright side – at least our grief has revealed the true colours of some people.

That went both ways because we also got to see who we could really count on – our tribe. Old relationships were strengthened, new friendships were made, and in our grief, we also learnt how to be more grief-aware ourselves. I believe that's the root of the problem – grief, similar to mental health, has always been a very taboo topic. Therefore, not many people know how to deal with it, both those going through it, and those supporting someone in their grief journey. That's why you end up with not just the first group, but also the last: those who stayed quiet or disappeared.

Again, I don't blame them – yes, it hurt, but there's no anger or resentment towards them because I get it! There were a few people who came up to me months later and explained that they never said anything because they were scared of saying the wrong thing. If I'm being honest, despite what I wrote earlier, I feel like I would rather people be in the first group than the fourth, because at least with the first group, I knew they were there.

That said, there were also some people who were the opposite: they were there in the first few months, then slowly disappeared. But that's life though, isn't it? People get busy, people move on. Some people are only in your life for a season, then seasons change. And that's why, if you happen to be one of the people in this group, I just want to assure you that there's nothing wrong with that.

In fact, I want to reassure anyone I know who is reading this book – it doesn't matter which group of people you feel you ended up in. This section is not about calling anyone out or making anyone feel guilty. It's about helping people to better understand grief, and hopefully become more grief-aware.

This section is for the people grieving: to help them know that they're not alone in what they're experiencing. It's about helping them to know that it's normal for people to come and go in their grief journey, and to help them know that it's not alright for anyone to gaslight them or treat them insensitively out of selfish intentions rather than a lack of awareness, regardless of whether or not they are family or a close friend.

This section is also for the people who are supporting someone who is grieving. Although I need to caution you again that everyone experiences grief differently, I hope this section helps to provide a glimpse into the mind of the griever. I hope it helps you with finding the right things to say (or not say!), to know how to be there for them, and what they might need from you.

Most importantly, this section is to help you realise that grief is deep and lingering, and that it often presents as an iceberg. Your loved one may not be as okay as they present themselves to be, so just be aware, be there, and give them a safe space so hopefully when they're ready, they'll share.

How I Feel

I know you're really worried,
I know you really care,
And I know you really do mean well,
When you ask me how I fare.

But there's a reason I don't want to talk,
Why I want to be left alone.
I don't think I can bear your grief,
I've got too much of my own.

And I don't like the awkwardness,
When you don't know what to say,
Then it's me comforting you,
Instead of it being the other way.

But even worse is when you try,
To tell me how to feel.
I know you have good intentions,
But this won't help me heal.

I don't want to hear you say,
That things happen for a reason,
Or that this pain and grief I feel,
Is only for a season.

Don't tell me about the grief you felt,
When you lost your spouse or parent.
I know you're just trying to relate with me,
But it is soooo immensely different.

Don't tell me to get out of bed.
Don't tell me to be strong.
Because I struggle just to hold myself,
Together for very long.

I know you're really worried,
I know you really care,
But if you really want to help me,
Just be patient and grief aware.

How Dare You

How dare you say we cut you out,
And make us out to be unkind?
After losing our child, do you really think,
You'd be the first thing on our minds?

You're the one who's selfish,
For thinking you come first,
Or thinking you're above our grief,
I don't know which is worse.

How dare you try to vilify us,
And say that we're at fault?
Who knew that grieving the child we lost,
Would be such a big assault?

Instead of understanding,
That we'd need time and space,
To process what was happening,
You overstepped your place.

How dare you talk behind our backs,
And spread evil, lies, and hate?
Don't you think that losing our child,
Was already a bad enough fate?

You have no idea what it feels like.
No, you haven't got a clue.
You never got to experience,
Your child passing before you do.

How dare you call us selfish,
After all that we've been through?
How dare you call us selfish?
I'd say the selfish one is you.

Not The Same

It's not a competition; it's not a game.
It's not worse; it's just not the same.

She's lost her spouse; he's lost his brother.
I've lost a child; you've lost your mother.

But even if I found another grieving mother,
Our story and the child we lost will never be like the other.

For how can you compare losing a child grown up,
To a child born with their eyes forever shut?

And the grief from the child lost in my belly,
Is different from the grief for the child I got to carry.

So you might know grief, but please don't claim,
To know my pain or make our grief the same.

Let's just agree that our pain's too big to name.
Yours is yours, and mine is mine; our grief is not the same.

You Don't Know

You see me out and about –
At the café, at the shops, running around town.
I smile and ask how you're going.
But you don't know that just yesterday I had a breakdown.

You see me come into work –
I join in the lunch talks, I make jokes, and I grin,
I seem organised, hard at work, productive –
But you don't know that most days I cry on the drive in.

You see me looking strong,
Carrying on, one foot after the other,
Standing tall, functioning as usual,
But you don't know how I struggle to hold it together.

You don't know what's behind my mask –
The pain I hide, the brokenness inside,
The battles that rage inside my mind,
How much and how often I've cried.

You don't know because I don't tell you.
I wasn't sure, I didn't think that you'd care.
It's not your problem after all, and I can't help but worry,
I'd just make you uncomfortable and think I overshare.

So you don't know,
And I pray you will never know this pain of mine.
But since you don't know,
Be thoughtful, be compassionate, be patient, be kind.

Say Their Name

Say their name; remember that they were here.
That you'll all forget them is something that we fear.
Hold onto every memory, every smile, and every tear.
Hold them in your hearts since we cannot hold them near.

Say their name; they existed; they were real.
It helps us to remember them; it helps us as we heal.
Talk to us about them – it's not that big a deal,
If we're feeling sensitive, we'll just tell you how we feel.

Say their name; cherish their time here on this earth.
It makes no difference whether or not they made it to a birth.
They still grew in our bellies; don't take away their worth.
Whatever time we had with them was filled with love and mirth.

Say their name; they're still part of our family.
Even if our dreams for them clashed with destiny.
We can't move on, so help us keep alive their memory,
Say their name, remember them, ensure their legacy.

To My Friends Who Remain

To all my friends who remain,
Thank you for being there.
Thanks for not giving up on me.
Thanks for showing that you care.

Thanks for being patient.
Thanks for giving me my space,
And allowing me to navigate,
This journey at my own pace.

Thank you for the messages,
And for checking in on me.
Thanks for all the food and prayers,
Your love, and company.

Thanks for sitting with me,
While I bare my heart and cry.
You might not know how to comfort me,
But I appreciate that you try.

But most of all, thank you for staying –
I know it might not have been easy to do.
Many have left, but you still remain,
So I'm grateful – truly grateful – to have friends like you.

Loss Before, or At Birth

Loss Before, or At Birth

As I covered in the introduction to this book, my motherhood journey didn't go as planned or expected. I've lost more children than I got to keep here on earth. I miscarried my very first baby, had my first son, had another suspected miscarriage, had my second son, then had my third son, Dorian, only to lose him unexpectedly at seven months for no known reason.

Despite having lost three babies, the grief I have for each of them is different. While the rest of this book is largely dedicated to Dorian, the grief I have over his loss, and grief in general, I wanted to include a little section in memory of my other two babies, and to all the other babies who were lost before/at birth.

The grief for my second miscarriage was weird as I didn't even realise I was pregnant until I was miscarrying, so I have no memories, and had no chance of forming a relationship with them. To be honest, I don't even know if you can call it grief, or if it's just a sorrow over the loss of something I didn't even know I had.

But the grief over my first miscarriage was very palpable. This was my first baby, and I had found out really early in the pregnancy. Even while my husband was still in disbelief and wanting me to get blood tests to confirm what the pregnancy stick tests were saying, I believed. I could feel all the changes in my body, and I was excited. Having just come out of a year of depression, anxiety, and mental health illness, this was my hope for a fresh start, especially as I found out just before New Year's Day.

We nicknamed this baby Poppy, because they were the size of a poppy seed when I first found out I was pregnant. I would talk to Poppy and rub my non-existent belly constantly in those few weeks. Even my husband had come out of his shock, and we were eagerly awaiting our first scan to get a glimpse of our little Poppy… except I miscarried the week leading up to the scan. The hardest part about this grief was the number of people who didn't understand that even though it was a miscarriage – and an early one at that – it was still loss. It was still grief.

For this section, I chose not to focus solely on the grief, as I feel like my poem 'Not The Same' from the previous 'Dear Everyone Else' section already captures that. Instead, I decided to explore the journey that follows a miscarriage or stillbirth*: from grief over the child you've lost, to the terror that grips you if you are blessed with another pregnancy, to the lingering love that remains in your heart for them – love that endures, even as you raise other children here on earth.

*I do want to note that I have never personally experienced a stillbirth, however I know many of you may have, so I didn't want you to feel excluded from this section if I just wrote it with early loss in mind. I know that I will never be able to understand your grief, and I would certainly never claim to know it, because as I've already mentioned, grief is never the same. With that said, I was inspired to write the poem 'Stolen' in honour of all the babies born sleeping, and I hope I've done it justice.

Poppy

You were the size of a poppy seed,
When I first found out about you.
You took me by surprise but oh,
How fast my love for you grew.

You were everything I wanted,
All that I'd dreamt of; my first.
You filled my heart with love –
So full, I thought it'd burst.

I didn't even know your gender –
Were you a boy or a girl?
It all happened so fast. I lost you,
Everything gone in a whirl.

I never got a chance to see you.
I have no pictures, no scans,
Nothing to remember you by,
Just broken dreams, unfulfilled plans.

But even now, when life's moved on,
I think about you still.
The child I never got to meet,
I love you; I always will.

Stolen

Bags were packed with all that we'd need,
Clothes to wear, something to do while you feed.

We were so ready and eager to meet you,
So close to the end, nearly made it through.

We didn't expect things would not turn out fine,
That we'd never quite make it to the finish line.

You looked so beautiful sound asleep.
Were it in our power to make your heart beat.

What should have been a joyous affair,
Was now filled with pain that was too hard to bear.

It hurts we never got to bring you home,
But your room still sits here, cold and alone.

All our plans, hopes, and dreams; our future broken.
Gone in an instant; just like you, they were stolen.

After

I'm trying but I'm struggling.
I can't seem to fully enjoy you.
I can't stop my mind from thinking,
What if I lose you too?

I'm terrified to bond with you,
In case my heart breaks again.
What if you go the way of your sibling?
I'm not sure I can handle more pain.

Your kicking brings me comfort,
To know you're alive and well.
But when it stops, I panic,
It's my own personal hell.

I'm watching everything I do,
I'm careful with what I eat.
Some people say I'm over-cautious,
But I'll do anything so we meet.

I'm struggling but I'm trying,
To stay positive, not fear disaster.
I really hope with you we'll get,
Our happily ever after.

Rainbow

Just because there is a rainbow,
Doesn't mean we forget the rain.
We might have your sibling now,
But losing you will always bring us pain.

A rainbow doesn't diminish,
All the storms that we went through.
Just like your sibling won't ever take away,
The love we have for you.

A rainbow is a promise,
A message of hope from above.
We like to think our rainbow came,
Because you protected them with your love.

And just like a rainbow is,
Always a wondrous sight,
So will your sibling always be,
A beautiful prism of your light.

Just because there is a rainbow,
Doesn't mean we forget the rain.
No matter how many siblings you get,
Your memory will always remain.

Milestones

Milestones

This book was written in the first year following Dorian's passing. Many people have said that the first year is usually the hardest because of all the "firsts" you'll have to endure. It's not just the big events and celebrations like first birthday, first Christmas, or first Mother's/Father's Day without them. It's also the little things: milestones like the first week, first month, and of course, first year without them; the first of many family photos that will never be complete again; the first day you didn't cry yourself to sleep.

Milestones we never asked for, instead of the milestones we should have had. That's what this section is about. We were robbed of so many milestones with Dorian, especially his first birthday, which I had planned – in faith – since he was still in my belly. There were so many things we never got to experience with him. Some of them we had no control over, but others we chose to put off because we never imagined we would never get the chance – how much we regret that now, but it's too late. Now, we commemorate instead of celebrate; each milestone and event now defiled and marred with grief.

I don't know if this will be forever; after all, it's only been a year since Dorian passed. That said, the thought of his second birthday, as well as Christmas later this year, both fill me with heaviness and dread. I know the grief will never fully leave, but I'd like to think that in time, events will become easier to endure, and marking off milestones won't stay at the forefront of our minds. Maybe one day, I'll follow up on this and let you know how it plays out.

You Would've Been One Today

You would've been one today.
Would you be walking yet?
I really can't say.
But I can imagine you,
pulling yourself to stand,
Maybe taking a few steps as we hold your hand.
And as you move slowly, step by step,
I can see that gummy grin as we cheer you on and clap.
Or maybe you'd have a tooth or two,
You might be teething;
Sucking your hand like you always do.

Would you be talking much?
Saying "Mama", "Dada", "bye bye", and such?
I wish I got the chance to hear you calling me.
What I would give to hear that,
Even if it was never-ending and repeatedly.
What would you have looked like now?
I wonder if you would have changed much, and if so, how?
Would you have grown quickly; big and tall?
And who would you have looked like, most of all?

I think about your personality…
Would you be wild and free,
Or would you be peaceful and happy?
Would you love to dance and sing?
What about art or books?
What would be your favourite thing?
Would you be fussy with food?
Or would you eat anything, as long as it's good?

You would've had your first taste of cake today.
You'd snuggle shyly into me
As everyone cheered "Hip, hip, hooray!"
We would've had a party to celebrate
All you are and all you would be.
But now instead we celebrate
Who you were; your beautiful memory.

You would've been one today.
You should've been one today.
I wish I knew why you couldn't stay.
It still hurts that you were taken away,
And I still miss you every day,
But we'll be together again, I pray…
One day.

Two Precious for This Earth

You should have been two today,
But you were too precious for this earth.
That has to be why you were called to heaven –
You were needed to join the angels up above.

I try to imagine what you would be like now,
And it hurts because I never got to know.
Would you be in the midst of the terrible twos?
Would your favourite word just be "no"?

Would you wake up really early?
Would you be sleeping through the night?
Would you crawl into our bed,
When you've had a nightmare or a fright?

Would you sit happily in your stroller,
Or still want to be carried everywhere?
I wonder about the sound of your voice,
If you'd have all your teeth, and the colour of your hair.

Every day I wonder what life would be like,
If you'd stayed with us, not just your memory.
But no matter how much time passes on earth,
You're still precious; you will always be precious to me.

Mother's Day

Even if your child is up in heaven above,
You are still a mother –
Your heart knows a mother's love.

Even if your child is no longer by your side,
You are still a mother –
Your angel is watching you with pride.

Even if your child can only be held in your heart,
You are still a mother –
You'll never be truly apart.

Even if Mother's Day feels like it's been defiled,
You will always be a mother,
They will always be your child.

Christmas

Christmas is supposed to be,
A time of peace, love, and joy.
But it doesn't feel so merry now,
That I've lost my little boy.

There's now an empty stocking,
There are now less presents to buy,
And the songs that used to bring me cheer,
Now make me want to cry.

There's always something missing,
Our Santa photos are incomplete,
And when we're having Christmas dinner,
There'll always be an empty seat.

Christmas used to light me up;
It was my favourite time of year.
But now the season's marred with pain,
And wishing you were here.

One Year Without You

One year without you,
Yet it feels like just yesterday,
When a piece of my heart along with
Your future were ripped away.

One year without you,
How did it go so fast?
I'm trying so hard to cling to
The memories of our past.

One year without you,
Many more yet to go.
Each as painful as the one before,
And filled with a you-sized hole.

One year without you,
Yet it feels like just yesterday.
It won't matter how much time passes,
This grief is here to stay.

Milestones We Never Asked For

One day without you turns to three,
Weeks turn into months.
Yet still we're left with all this pain,
And grief we must confront.

Now, milestones like your birthdays,
We don't get to celebrate,
But instead, the day you passed away,
We're left to commemorate.

We were robbed of all your milestones,
Like when you started walking,
And things like you starting school,
Your graduation, and your wedding.

Instead, we get these milestones:
Our first Christmas without you,
A hole in our family portrait,
The first year we made it through.

A family affair without crying,
Seeing people you never got to meet.
Your baby book that's been finished,
But will always be incomplete.

Learning to forgive ourselves,
Let go of guilt, "move on",
Organising all your things,
Accepting that you're gone.

Milestones we never wanted,
Milestones we never asked for,
But these are the milestones that we have,
Milestones we're stuck with forevermore.

Faith Musings

Faith Musings

> *"I can't imagine how you're still getting out of bed/ standing/functioning."*
> *"I don't know how you do it."*
> *"You must be so strong."*
> *"You are such an inspiration."*

These (or variations of these) are all things that many people have said to me after Dorian's passing. The truth is, I don't know how I could be or do it all either…if it weren't for my faith.

My family and I became Christians when I was in high school. But if I'm honest, I believe my "real" faith journey didn't start until after my first miscarriage, and it grew exponentially in the last couple of years through my journey with Dorian. I won't go into detail (that's a story for another time!), and I've covered the gist of it in the introduction to this book, so I won't repeat myself now, but boy, was it a faith journey!

If I thought that my pregnancy with Dorian was a test of faith, and our life together a test of patience, then my grief journey has turned out to be a test of both, amplified. A few people have asked me how I could still believe in God after what I've been through. This is a tricky one to explain, and harder still for someone to understand if they don't believe in God themselves – but the short answer is, how can I not?

Despite everything I've been through, despite my worst fear being realised, God has shown me constantly that He was there, and still is here with me especially in my grief. God has been my provider, getting us through months of unpaid bereavement leave, and even now providing us with what we need, sometimes before we even realise we need it. God is my comfort, speaking to me and giving me visions of my little boy in heaven. God is my strength, keeping me going instead of wasting away in bed. God is my peace, helping me survive the trauma and mental attacks despite my mental health history and having previously been taken out by lesser things than the loss of my son.

God's ways and thoughts are higher. Even though I don't have an answer to why God would let Dorian die, and even though I may never get an answer to that on this earth, I continue to believe that God is good, and that ultimately, He will work all things for good. Because I have seen His hand in my life – and that of my family's – for as long as I have known God, not just in these past couple of years.

God understands sacrifice and grief more than I ever could, and He is not asking me to give up my grief or believe that Dorian's passing is a good thing. Dorian's passing will never be a good thing, but there have been good things that have come from it since then. All God is asking me to do is trust that He will continue to restore and create beauty from the ashes, and keep holding on and believing that I will see Dorian again one day. And when I do, we will have forever.

I owe everything I have to God, including this book, which you wouldn't be holding in your hands right now if it weren't for Him – His giftings and Spirit working in and through me, and some beautiful people that He very timely placed in my life to help me send this book out into the world. This particular section is especially dedicated to God and my relationship with Him: my questions and wrestles, my prayers and pleas, and ultimately, my continued trust and faith in God.

At the end of the day, I wouldn't be standing, let alone functioning, if it weren't for Him. To God be the glory, forever and ever. Amen.

Beauty From Ashes

What once was, now is gone.
The life we had, now we mourn.
Where once was hope, now there's despair.
There's no more drive; we no longer care.
But from the ashes, You will mould,
A crown of beauty for all to behold.
You'll adorn us with happiness and praise,
Your spirit of joy in us You'll raise.
You'll nurture us from acorn to tree,
A display of Your glory for all to see.
Though our flesh and heart may fail,
You'll give us strength so we can prevail.
Our hearts we thought broken beyond repair,
You'll heal and bind all our wounds with care.
You'll wipe away every tear from our lashes,
You'll restore and give us beauty from the ashes.
We trust You because You have called us precious,
So, we'll wait for Your beauty from our ashes.

You Said

You said You'd heal and You'd restore,
You alone can conquer death.
So why did You not save my child,
When I pled with all my breath?

You said You'd rescue and protect,
That You'd satisfy with long life.
But why didn't Your angels guard us,
From disaster, harm, and strife?

You said, "Have faith"; I know I did –
Bigger than a mustard seed.
Why wasn't it enough to save my child?
What more did You need?

You said You'd do whatever I asked,
If I asked it in Your name,
But You didn't, even though I begged,
And others did the same.

You said You had plans to prosper;
Plans for a future and hope.
But it seems like pain, grief, and trauma,
Have become my life's constant trope.

You said that You'd be with me,
And comfort me when I cry.
But I wish You'd share your reasons,
And answer when I ask why.

But I know You said to trust You;
Higher are Your ways and thoughts.
So I'll leave my burdens at the cross,
And let You call the shots.

You said You keep your promises,
That You'll make all things for good.
So I know You'll stay here by my side,
Just like You said You would.

You said be strong, take heart,
And find my hope in You.
And so I'll wait, and I'll keep faith,
That You'll help me make it through.

Restoration – Your Way

You said You will restore my life,
But I can't see how that will be.
I just don't know what restoration,
Could look like for someone like me.

I see people who have lost their partners,
In time they might meet someone new.
I see people who have lost their babies,
Get their rainbow child, maybe even a few.

But it won't work that way for me,
And that's why I struggle when I pray.
I can't replace the child I lost,
And I don't want more kids anyway.

I know those people aren't replacing,
The loved ones that they grieve,
I know that their hearts still hold sadness,
Grief is still in the new stories they weave.

I know Job got more kids and possessions,
You restored him double all things.
But I don't see how there's a way to create,
A new story for me; a new happy ending.

Because there's a part of me missing,
And nothing can replace it exactly,
But I won't even have a different piece,
That might patch up the hole left inside me.

But You promised me restoration,
So I trust that You can and You will,
I'm sure it'll look nothing like what I expect,
But what matters is it fits Your bill.

So I'll keep believing that in the end,
I'll be restored though I can't see how.
I know what awaits me in eternity,
Will be better than what I have now.

Yours, Not Mine

I asked You to take this cup from me,
But Your will was done, not mine.
So I just have to trust that in the end,
It will come good for Your glory divine.

For I know that ultimately,
Your plans will prosper, not harm me.
So I'll trust in You faithfully,
That You'll guard me, and You'll guide me.

And though I cannot understand,
How You could make this work for good,
I have to trust that You'll redeem,
Just like You said You would.

For Your Word stands true forever,
And Your thoughts and ways are higher.
So I'll follow you wherever;
Help me accomplish what You desire.

My Reason

When I'm at the end of my rope,
In You I find my strength and hope.

When everything seems to be falling apart,
In You I find comfort for my aching heart.

When I'm lost and can't see the path ahead,
It's You I turn to when I'm afraid.

When I feel I can't go on anymore,
In You I trust to heal and restore.

When everything about me just feels broken,
It's Your truth I'll hold fast to; the words You've spoken.

When all that surrounds me is loss and grief,
It's You where I go to find peace and reprieve.

Through every storm and every season,
In You I trust; You are my reason.

Moving On
(But Never Gone)

Moving On (But Never Gone)

Finally, this last section is about "What next?". What happens in the months and years following the loss of your loved one? How do you move on and live the rest of your life? What does moving on look like? Can you even move on?

I think I wrote this section largely for me; not just for you. This section is my reminder that it is normal to worry and be scared of what the future will look like with grief. It is my reassurance that I will never forget Dorian, and that even though I may never truly heal or move on from his loss, I will find my own version of "moving on" in time. Above all, this section contains hopes for myself and my future; that I will overcome, and even if my grief never goes away, that in time it will become easier to bear.

I know your grief journey is not easy. I know that sometimes it seems too hard to bear. I know there may be moments when you feel so alone, and nobody understands what you're going through. I hope you know that you're not alone. I hope this section encourages you and helps you find the light in the darkness. Most of all, I hope this section gives you the courage to hope again, and reminds you that your loved one will never truly be gone.

Holding On

Holding on to all these things,
That might seem trivial and small,
Because I'm scared to let them go,
I don't want to lose it all.

There's a memory attached,
To each item that you once had.
That's why it's hard to let them go –
I want to remember the good and bad.

I've tried to preserve your clothes,
Your things, the pillow that you laid on.
I just can't seem to let them go,
Though your smell on them's long gone.

I know keeping all your things seems silly,
But I'm holding on because I'm afraid.
I don't want to let you go,
I can't let your memory fade.

Moving On

It starts off slowly at first,
Then almost overnight you find,
Everyone around you has moved on,
But you're still stuck and left behind.

To you it feels like just yesterday,
When your heart was ripped in two.
But to everyone else it was forever ago,
They've now got other things to do.

You can't really blame them though,
They have their own lives to lead.
After all, it wasn't their grief to bear,
So it's easier to pay it no heed.

But you know inside your heart,
That no matter what you do,
You'll carry this grief with you always,
There's no real "moving on" for you.

For you, moving on will look different.
Moving on won't mean to forget,
But to carry on doing life each day,
And letting go of guilt and regret.

Moving on might even be as simple,
As getting out of bed every day.
And not getting triggered or crying,
Over the things others might do or say.

Whatever moving on may look like for you,
Just remember that it's not a race.
Moving on will look different for everyone.
Don't stress; just move at your own pace.

Never Gone

People say that time will heal,
That in time you'll start to move on,
But I'm not sure how many understand,
That your pain will never truly be gone.

Time will never heal these wounds,
They just get a little easier to bear,
But no matter how much time passes,
You'll still have bad days here and there.

Your pain itself doesn't lessen,
Your love certainly won't go away,
But it's your strength and resilience,
That will grow bit by bit every day.

In time, some memories may start to fade,
But take comfort even as you mourn,
And know they'll always be in your heart,
They'll never truly be gone.

One Day

One day those empty seats won't be,
So glaringly obvious anymore,
Even if family photos stay incomplete,
And still hit that spot that's sore.

Sometimes you worry that one day,
Their memories might start to fade.
People will say that could never happen,
But know it's valid to be afraid.

One day you might be able to talk about it,
And find your eyes stay dry.
But even if that only lasts a day,
Know that it's okay to cry.

One day you'll feel less broken,
And there won't be so much pain,
Even if there'll always be a piece missing,
And you never feel whole again.

One day you will find strength again.
One day you'll start to heal.
And one day you'll take comfort that,
The love you had was real.

But even if that one day never comes,
Know there's nothing wrong with you.
I'm still waiting for that day myself,
But together, we'll make it through.

My Hopes for You

I hope your light comes back.
I hope you build a new you.
I hope you find peace and happiness,
In all that you choose to do.

I hope you'll stop blaming yourself,
And accept you did nothing wrong.
I hope you find the key to healing,
Was inside you all along.

I hope one day you'll start to ask,
"What now?" instead of "Why?",
And work to leave behind for them,
A legacy that will never die.

I hope you realise how strong you are,
You battled grief and didn't succumb.
I hope one day that you'll look back,
And realise how far you've come.

I hope you know they're watching,
And that they're so proud of you.
And I hope you know they'll always,
Always be a part of you.

Afterword

Dear Reader,

I don't know who or what brought you to my book. I don't know your story and I don't want to assume, but given the content of my book, I feel it would be safe to say that whatever your story is, you have known the pain of grief and loss. Or perhaps you know – or are supporting – someone who is going through their own grief journey. And if you happen to also be a mother who has lost her child/children, my heart goes out to you all the more.

Whoever you are, and whatever your story is, I hope that my book has now made you feel more seen. I hope you know that you are not alone, and that you are not crazy for feeling whatever you feel. I know there are no words to take away the pain, but I hope my words have at least brought you some comfort and solidarity.

A dear friend told me, "Your grief won't get smaller, but the container you have to hold it will get keep getting bigger in time."

It is my hope and prayer that in every moment of every day, you find the strength you need to keep going.

I hope you find courage in yourself to face the world and all the unexpected triggers (and even the expected ones!) that your day may bring. And I hope that in time, those triggers will start to trigger less and less, and that your reactions to them become smaller and less overwhelming.

Most of all, I hope you find a purpose in your pain. I hope you find light in the darkness. And more than that, you can eventually become that light for someone else.

Thank you for opening your heart to my words – it is no easy feat to pour my vulnerability onto pages and put it out there for the world to see. If you feel so inclined, I would love to know your thoughts, so please feel free to email them through to hello@lynnvincent.com.au. I will try my best to personally respond to each one, but if not, I will certainly cherish reading them.

Love and prayers,
Lynn

Acknowledgments

First and foremost, *God*. This book was only made possible because of the gifts He has blessed me with, His Holy Spirit working in and through me, and His guidance and provision. He opened the doors and made a way for this book to become a reality - to God be the glory.

My husband, *Clarke* – for being my sounding board during the entire writing and publishing process, and for reading through my poems even when it brought out all the emotions. Thank you for always supporting me in everything I do, and most of all, thank you for being my rock. I love you.

My parents, *Phow* and *Lorraine* – for encouraging my writing since I was a child, for supporting and even pushing me to accomplish my dream of writing a book, especially a book of poetry. Thank you for always believing in me and being so proud of me. I love you, and I am lucky to have parents like you.

Lisa – for being a friend, counsellor, and safe space. You are a rock and an inspiration, and you have played such an important role in my motherhood and grief journey. I am so grateful for everything you have done and blessed to have you in my life.

Amy – for sitting for hours with me in my heartbreak and tears, for your support and prayers, and most of all, for loving my family as we are. And thank you for introducing me to…

Sue – thank you for all your advice, support, and encouragement with my writing. Most of all, thank you for helping me get my very first book out into the world. God knew I needed you, so thank you for answering His calling and starting that Writers Group in faith, where you introduced me to…

Julieann – thank you for your wealth of knowledge and advice. Most of all, thank you for your love and kindness in helping me get this book published. You were the blessing I needed to get me over the finish line, and I pray God returns that blessing to you ten-fold!

Lisa-Marie – for your beautiful designs. Not only has your cover so perfectly captured the essence of my book, but your illustrations have helped bring colour and life to my pages! I have no words, except that you absolutely nailed it!

And last, but furthest from the least, *my two boys* who remain – don't ever doubt that I love you just as much as your brother, Dorian. You are the reasons I am still here and fighting every single day.

About The Author

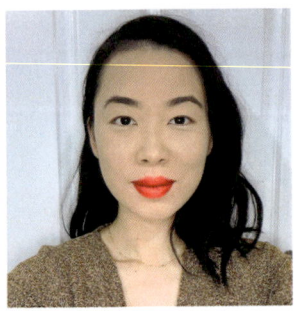

Lynn Vincent is the imperfect mother of three boys: one neurodivergent, one in the chaos of toddlerhood, and one who went to heaven too soon. Grief has been embedded in her motherhood journey with more children lost than alive.

She's had two miscarriages, and in July 2024, her youngest son, Dorian, passed away suddenly and unexpectedly at seven months old, following a trip to ED from reasons that we may never know on this earth. Between that and her history of depression, anxiety, and mental health illness, she really should not be standing here today let alone functioning, but by God's grace she is.

Her grief reignited her passion for writing as a creative outlet and mental health therapy, as well as her childhood dream of writing a book. As it turns out, her passion and dreams aligned with God's calling on her life, leading her to use her writing gifts and life's stories to help encourage and inspire others, specifically other mums. Her mission is to help light up the darkness, inspire, and help other mums feel seen and less alone.

Besides writing poetry and books, she regularly shares her musings on life, motherhood, and mental health – intertwined with her faith and grief – through her blog and social media. If you'd like to read more of her works, stay updated with new book releases, or follow along her motherhood and grief journey, you can find her online in the following places:

Website: www.lynnvincent.com.au
Blog: Mother | Write | Inspire
Instagram: @lynnvincent.writes

www.ingramcontent.com/pod-product-compliance
Lightning Source LLC
Chambersburg PA
CBRC091204070526
44583CB00011B/200